A Private Commission
New Verses by Shakespeare

A PRIVATE COMMISSION
New Verses by Shakespeare

Peter Levi

MACMILLAN
LONDON

For Deirdre

First published 1988 by
MACMILLAN LONDON LIMITED
4 Little Essex Street London WC2R 3LF
and Basingstoke

Associated companies in Auckland,
Delhi, Dublin, Gaborone, Hamburg,
Harare, Hong Kong, Johannesburg,
Kuala Lumpur, Lagos, Manzini,
Melbourne, Mexico City, Nairobi, New
York, Singapore and Tokyo

ISBN 0–333–47655–7

Designed by Robert Updegraff
Typeset by Wyvern Typesetting Limited
Bristol
Printed in Great Britain by
St Edmundsbury Press Limited
Bury St Edmunds, Suffolk
Bound by Dorstel Press, Harlow
Member of BPCC PLC

Introduction

T HESE VERSES ARE unpublished, with an exception to which I shall refer. They come from a manuscript in the Huntington Library in California where they survived on a loose page attached to a private masque by Shakespeare's friend John Marston. We know that they belong to the same occasion of an engagement ceremony at a private party. In preparing a biography of Shakespeare I had already noticed the importance of his relationship with the younger Marston, and therefore I became interested in the Huntington manuscript. As for the attribution of the verses to Shakespeare, I have brooded over this for more than a year; I am now anxious to place the argument as it stands before the public, and to print the text which I believe that Shakespeare wrote or had a hand in writing. Readers must judge for themselves.

By publishing the verses in this way, we are inevitably removing them from the context in Shakespeare's life in which they make most sense. What follows after this paragraph is simply one of the appendices to my *Life and Times of William Shakespeare* (now in the press), in which subordinate position they will take their lowly place. They are not a very great find, but I believe they are genuinely Shakespeare's, and even if they were not they are interesting enough to detain attention. I have left the further investigation which must now take place to the professional scholars who will be happy to undertake it.

I have already been told that there is more to be said than I knew about the precise date of the private celebration, and that there are relevant letters I had not read, but I leave these points to be made by their discoverer. I have also noticed that the activities of a forger with a special interest in Marston have been traced in papers in the same collection, but I greatly doubt whether the signature on these verses is a forgery, for reasons which I will state. No doubt this matter will be scientifically settled. Even if the signature turned out to have been tampered with, there is still a strong case that Shakespeare is the author of these verses.

Peter Levi
9 January 1988

The Background

I HAVE PURSUED a personal interest in the private commissions Shakespeare may have undertaken for their literary as well as their social interest, because more even than the theatre, with its largely nameless audience, they show poetry in a precise social context to which it must adapt. Shakespeare's own inscribed gravestone is an example, and the very different inscription on his wall monument shows by contrast how intimately and directly he could speak in poetry. So I ought not to have been surprised when this interest led me, by way of a private masque written by Shakespeare's younger friend John Marston, to the discovery of some unpublished verses which I find it impossible not to attribute to Shakespeare. They are comparatively minor verses for a social occasion. Before dealing with them, it will be better to say a little more about his private commissions.

Until recently the only evidence that Shakespeare ever worked on private commissions from the aristocracy was the stray fact of an entry in an account book at Belvoir Castle for 1613. 'Item 31 Martii to Mr. Shakespeare in gold about my Lord's impreso 44s. To Richard Burbadge for painting and making it in gold 44s.' An *impreso* is an emblem with a motto precisely like the ones Shakespeare invents for *Pericles* (act 2, scene ii) and it seems likely that the Earl of Rutland, who was Southampton's friend and fellow-prisoner in the Tower until 1603, had thought of Shakespeare because of this scene and that Shakespeare brought in Burbage as a painter.

The 1613 royal tournament at Belvoir does not sound like a success. 'The day', wrote Sir Henry Wotton to a friend, 'fell out wet, to the disgrace of many fine plumes. . . . The rest were contented with bare *imprese*, whereof some were so dark that their meaning is not yet understood. . . .' Lord Pembroke presented 'a small, exceeding white pearl, and the words *solo candore valeo*'. Lord Montgomery had 'a sun casting a glance on the side of a pillar, and the beams reflecting with the motto *splendente refulget*'. To judge from the examples in *Pericles*, Shakespeare's will have been better. Pericles presented 'A wither'd branch, that's only green at top' with the motto '*In hac spe vivo*' – In this hope I live. These *imprese* (*impreso* is a wrong form) are not the same as the heraldic devices on shields, since Pericles has no shield: they are handed to the Princess by each knight's attendant, but Pericles has no attendant. The audience is not shown the *imprese*, which is why the Princess describes them to her father.

Shakespeare undertook another private commission in 1607, which has been overlooked. It is not only a unique pleasure to present unknown verses by Shakespeare in print for the first time, but also a little alarming, because modern attempts to attribute little-known or unknown works to his authorship have often misfired. The 1607 poems are at least new; the manuscript has an excellent provenance, but it appears that the verses had scarcely been read since soon after 1607 until December 1986. In itself the signature 'W.S.' may mean anything or nothing, but the case for the signature of these poems is very much stronger. Most of the marginal works attributed to Shakespeare are simply not good enough to be written by him; these verses are minor work, but a few of them are certainly good enough, and the whole series seems to have been written by a single author. Without the signature one would suspect some close disciple of Shakespeare, if one hardly dared to suggest the poet himself, but given the signature little or no doubt remains.

The scene is a formal ceremony of present-giving at a country house, a ritualized, almost a masque-like performance of a familiar action, enacted between close friends and members of a family with an audience of the same kind. This is a ceremony of friends and neighbours, an extended family and kinship group, to celebrate a most important binding link: an engagement to be married. There are fourteen present-givers, a number deliberately chosen, I suppose, to represent the fourteen lines of a sonnet. The presents are similar, so perhaps one person payed for them all; certainly one person arranged the entire ceremony from the time when the presents were commissioned, as soon as the marriage was arranged. That is the person who employed Shakespeare; and I take it to be Alice, the dowager Countess of Derby. The engagement is that of her eldest daughter, Anne, to Lord Chandos.

There is not more than one small textual problem in these poems. Scholars will need to consult the manuscript for themselves, and no doubt it will be published in facsimile. I have chosen to reproduce it in modern spelling for ordinary readers, though specialized scholars will undoubtedly pore over its original spelling and punctuation. There is no reason to think the manuscript is autograph: it was intended to be a clean copy for use at the Earl of Huntingdon's house at Ashby-de-la-Zouch in Leicestershire. I do not suppose that the signature was added until it arrived there, certainly not by the copyist. But one or two strange spellings do suggest Shakespeare's Warwickshire accent, not unlike a modern Staffordshire accent, unless we are to think a local copyist altered these spellings. The same possibility occurs here and there in his dramatic works. Here he calls Lady Compton *Lady Coumpton* and spells coloured *coulored*. An amethyst is an *amatist*, a spelling used earlier by alchemists, but also by Sidney in his *Arcadia*; from 1596 or so, and certainly from 1611 (the date of the authorized Bible) onwards, it would have been ignorant and old-fashioned.

The occasion of the masque and the present-giving is the same because both involve the same people. Lady Derby had planned her visit to Ashby the previous winter, but she was stopped by snow, as Marston says in his *Entertainment* for the end of July 1607:

> For scarce her Chariot cut the easy earth
> And journied on, when winter with cold breath
> Crosseth her way. Her borrowed hair doth shine
> With Glittering Icicles all crystalline,
> Her brows were periwigg'd with softer snow,
> Her russet mantle fring'd with Ice below
> Sat stiffly on her back. . . .

I am not sure why her hair is borrowed, unless as a goddess, and one hopes that the rest of the picture is exaggerated. The seventeenth century thought of Ashby as a long way north: Charles Cotton wrote in similar terms to Sir Aston Cockayne, and 1607 was the year of 'a great frost' long remembered. It was also the year of the execution of the Derbyshire witches at Bakewell. In late July, Lady Derby was greeted with music at 'the Park corner', again as she entered the park 'treble cornets reported to one another', and suddenly she came to 'an Antique gate' where she was entertained with Marston's verse. The Earl of Huntingdon, Chief Forester of Leicester forest, was 'the high silvan that commands these woods', and his wife, who was Alice Derby's daughter, was 'his bright Nymph fairer than Queen of floods'. The learned entertainment continued indoors, with music and singing, Shakespearean fairy talk, and the presentation of 'a very curious and rich waistcoat'.

Some plumes 'of Carnation and white' for knights seem to derive from Jonson's *Hymenaei* (1606), and may well have been the same plumes that he used at Court, since two of the dancers are the same. The most learned bit of Marston's masque is a list of the obscure Latin names of the sons of Mercury, which he took from the *Mythologia* of Natalis Cornes. It is fascinating to observe that Shakespeare was better informed than Marston, since the masque gives 'Auctolius' as one of them. Perhaps it was this queer list that stirred Shakespeare to look up Ovid's *Metamorphoses*, which gives Autolycus, son of Mercury, power over thievery. Autolycus was an Arcadian, and therefore doubly suitable for his role in *The Winter's Tale*.

The Argument

I N THE COURSE of reading the necessary and vast material for a life of Shakespeare, I became interested in a possible influence on him of a younger and lesser poet, the satirist John Marston, and in Shakespeare's obvious influence on him. It is a pleasing thought that the first person to notice this connection was Rupert Brooke, and that, had he lived, he might well have found what I have found. I was also particularly curious about masques and private performances of every kind, which are marginal and yet important in the history of the public theatre, particularly under the Stuarts. I therefore consulted Arnold Davenport's *Poems of John Marston* (1961), which he completed just before his early and sudden death at the age of forty-eight in 1958. Davenport's main interest was in satirists, but in editing Marston he had to deal with *The Entertainment of the Dowager Countess of Derby*, written by Marston and performed in late July or early August 1607 for the engagement of her eldest daughter, Anne, to Lord Chandos. Here, as often elsewhere, I follow Davenport's suggestions, which are well argued in his introduction.

The only full manuscript of the masque that survives is in the Huntington Library in California (E.L.34.B.9), to the Director of which I am very grateful for permission to publish this text. A manuscript of part of the masque is in the British Library (Sloane 848), dated by its copyist 1607, August, but that is hasty and useless. Marston refers in a letter to having

9

copies hastily made. The Huntington manuscript was once in the collection of the Bridgewater family, and presumably of the first Lord Bridgewater, John, the son of Thomas Egerton, Lord Brackley, who was Lord Chancellor and the second husband of Alice Derby. To the Huntington–Bridgewater manuscript of the masque was attached a stray leaf, which survived with it and is still with it. Davenport used the stray leaf as a key to unlock the secrets of the masque, because it consists of a series of short poems, often no more than four lines each, recited by ladies, whose names are given, at some sort of ceremonial present-giving to the bride. The presents were emblematic, and the poems are like riddles: all the presents seem to be jewels or such things, but it is sometimes hard, now that we have only the words, to guess what they were.

The stray leaf is headed 'Ashridge Library', in what looks to me like an early nineteenth-century hand, with the catalogue note F–4–3. Ashridge was an Egerton house in Hertfordshire which passed to Lord Brownlow in the nineteenth century. This estate survives, in the hands of the National Trust, as some fine woods on the edge of the Chilterns near Ivenhoe Beacon, not far from Tring and Mentmore. John Egerton, the first Lord Bridgewater, settled there sixteen miles from his father's and Alice Derby's house at Harefield. The old Ashridge was a house in which Queen Elizabeth had lived as a young woman, but it was replaced in 1808 by a new building in extravagantly 'Elizabethan' style, just about the time that Marston's *Entertainment* first attracted attention.

H. J. Todd printed some extracts from that in 1801 in the fifth volume of his *Works of Milton*, and the same extracts were reprinted by J. Nichols in his Progresses of James I in 1828. As an Egerton manuscript, our stray leaf and Marston's masque formed part of the Bridgewater collection, and must have belonged to that library since August 1607, since Thomas Egerton was (as I have said) Alice Derby's second husband.

The papers of her daughters and granddaughters, who took other titles, would not survive in this collection. The whole library was sold to Mr Huntington in 1917 through Sir Montague Barlow of Sotheby's without an auction. The sale was to meet death duties, sales by auction being hazardous at the time. The library as sold included an early *Hamlet*, a 1600 quarto of *Titus Andronicus*, and a copy of Milton's *Comus* belonging to one of the boys who acted in it, which was later unfortunately sold off as a duplicate. The manuscripts from Ashridge had been moved to Bridgewater House in London, presumably by the Duke of Sutherland, who inherited as nephew from the last Duke of Bridgewater in the early nineteenth century. They were probably moved at the time of the rebuilding of Ashridge.

I should make one further point here. John Payne Collier, a famous forger of Shakespearean documents, had access to the Bridgewater papers in the 1830s and 1840s. I did not know that he ever saw this stray leaf, but he handled Marston's masque, and its title-page for his purposes. Had he seen this leaf, I was sure he would have pounced on it, since he did pounce on genuine documents as well as giving publicity to those he invented. At the last moment, I discovered that Collier did attribute a manuscript to Shakespeare in his *New Particulars*, but Chambers does not mention it in his catalogue of known or supposed Collier forgeries. I assume that these few poems were beyond his capacity and too subtle for him. After some uncertainty, I dismiss the possibility that Collier wrote or interfered with these poems. It remains doubtful whether he touched the signature.

Sir Edward Dering's manuscript of Shakespeare's *Henry IV*, edited By J. O. Halliwell-Phillips in 1845, contained not a stray leaf but 'a slip of paper' that recorded the names of country-house actors in *The Spanish Curate*, perhaps as early as 1619, the year in which Sir Edward was knighted (1845 edition, p. xiv). One of these actors is called Mr Donne. It is not impossible, indeed given the company it might seem likely, that this was John Donne the poet, but the poet became Dean of St Paul's in 1621, so the performance of *The Spanish Curate* would have to have been in 1620, or very soon before or after that year. The Dering manuscript itself, which is an adapted *Henry IV, Parts 1* and *2*, is equally hard or still harder to date. It appears to have been made by a genuine poet, since it contains at least one excellent joke at Falstaff's expense that occurs in no other text: 'I'll take say of ye', which means drawing the knife along a deer's belly to see how fat he is. The other actors in the *Curate*, apart from Dering, were Sir T. Wotton, Sir Warham St Leger, Robert Heywood, Thomas Slender, Mr Donne and Mr Kemp. The same slip of paper carries a second, slightly different list for the same characters: F. Manouch, John Carlile, Jack of the Buttery, and George Perd are the new names, making ten instead of nine. These lists offer an analogy to our ceremony.

The new Shakespeare poems are a family manuscript commemorating a family occasion. Arnold Davenport was interested only in the occasion and in the names, which are certainly fascinating. The more important present-givers are an interrelated family group from the higher aristocracy, the grandest of all being the first named, the widow of Ferdinando Strange, Earl of Derby, who is said to have died by poisoning after an attempt to involve him in an intrigue against Queen Elizabeth, which he spurned. His sad story was pieced together by Christopher Devlin in *Hamlet's Divinity* (1963). Alice Derby was patroness to Spenser and to Milton, and now it seems to Shakespeare as well. She is buried in Harefield Church in Middlesex in one of the most beautiful tombs in England, a few miles across the fields from where I was born. The daughter who became Anne Chandos later married Lord

Castlehaven, a sadistic sexual pervert who was publicly executed in his wife's and Lady Derby's lifetime: that catastrophe is the background to Milton's *Comus*. The little ceremony of the present-giving was not the prelude to a happy life.

The poetry on the stray leaf is in Elizabethan 'secretary' hand. It is not a particularly easy example, but with the possible exception of one word it can be read. The names opposite each few lines are in italic and therefore very much easier. My own suspicion, which is not meant to be insulting, is that Arnold Davenport saw that it was not Marston, who wrote an elaborate, rather beautiful italic hand, and never seriously examined it. The names and the verses are probably written by the same person; it would be common practice at this period to use both types of writing in a variety of combinations.

When I had begun to decipher the poems I thought it just possible that they might really be by Shakespeare: those I first read were at least good enough not absolutely to rule him out, though they are only minor verses for a private occasion, much the kind of verse that occurs in love-notes in his comedies. He does use the same verse form for that sort of purpose. Marston uses it in his dedication to Lady Derby, but much less well, as one would expect. I think Marston is imitating these verses.

It was the signature that altered everything. I had gone to Mr R. E. Alton of St Edmund Hall in Oxford to have the handwriting examined and properly deciphered; I knew that the hand was not Shakespeare's, and not the famous 'Hand D' of *Sir Thomas More* which has been attributed to Shakespeare, but that still left a wide-open field, and there were lines I was unable to read. Mr Alton is not responsible for my conclusions, but without his help I would have been lost. The signature is very odd. Davenport records it as 'W:SR:', which suggests Shakespeare among other possibilities. In fact someone has played with the signature, writing first 'W:Sʰ:' and then changing that without erasure to 'W:Sℛ:', suggesting both (certainly) 'R' and (perhaps) 'K'. In a manuscript of this date, when William Shakespeare was a famous and much-imitated poet, 'W.Sh[K]R' is certainly meant to mean Shakespeare.

There is no question of forgery, because the signature, though nothing else on the stray sheet, is in the hand of John Marston. It is clear from the little poems that they are not Marston's own work, but he was there, and he knew Shakespeare, and when he signs this copy with the poet's initials I think we must believe him. His hand in the odd signature is immediately recognizable by his peculiar 'S', and the 'W' is his 'W'. I am sure this text would have been recognized as Shakespeare's long ago if anyone had bothered to read it in modern times, or at least at any time since Greg's facsimile publication of Marston's hand. Lady Hunsdon's 'O be not proud, though. . . .' oddly recalls a sonnet by Donne, a member of the Egerton household from 1597 to 1602. The same Donne sonnet echoes a Shakespeare sonnet. Lady Berkeley's 'fire and air' recalls *Antony and Cleopatra* at just the time when Shakespeare had been writing it, and a number of other lines recall his work in other ways. The poems are uneven, though some are very good, but I do not wish to make them out to be more important than they are. It is conceivable that some of the ladies wrote their own verses.

They do in small ways alter our view of Shakespeare, because here he is playful, and reveals a frontier of verse with life and of his own comedies with life. That may be thought to throw some light on the sonnets. Then one is interested in his accepting a private commission, and in his never bothering to print these verses. His other undoubted private commission was his riddling emblem for the Earl of Rutland mentioned above. These verses in their way are also emblematic.

Shakespeare's early friend Thomas Combe translated an emblem book from the French, and Daniel translated emblem verses from the Italian.

The poetry of emblem books veers between the two opposite poles of originality, which leads towards the amazing conceits of 'metaphysical' verse in the later seventeenth century (though much earlier abroad), and convention, a solid basis of familiar symbolism which permits a descant on a scarcely stated theme. An example of the second of the two tendencies is to be found in a sonnet on a portrait of Queen Elizabeth at Hampton Court, preserved in W. Hutton's guide to that palace (1897) and reprinted as the first poem in John Holloway's *Oxford Book of Local Verse* (1987). Its symbols or emblems are the swallow, the weeping stag, and the tree or love-tree. The same polarity and the same familiar emblems are to be found in these new poems and elsewhere in the works of Shakespeare.

The persons and the occasion are suggestive. It looks as if Shakespeare himself was not present. Did he not bother or was he not asked? Did Marston get him the job, or did he (more likely) get it for Marston? His obvious point of contact was with Lady Hunsdon, whose husband had been his employer in the Chamberlain's Men. But this group of people may add slightly to the case often made in the past, that Shakespeare as a young man worked for Lord Strange's Men. In that case Ferdinando's widow had probably followed his fortunes. For her, unhappy lady, this stray page of writing has an unexpected meaning after so long. It makes her beyond question the most interesting patroness in the entire history of English literature: Spenser, Shakespeare, Milton. You cannot do better than that.

The Poems

(Huntington Ms. E.L.34.B.9)

LADY DERBY

As this is endless, endless be your joy,
Value the wish, but not the wisher's toy;
And for one blessing past God send you seven
And in the end the endless joys of heaven.
Till then let this be all your cross,
To have [?share] discomfort of your loss.

LADY HUNTINGDON

Alas, your fortune should be better,
Still must your servant be your debtor:
Sure nothing equals your desert
Except your servant's faithful heart.

LADY HUNSDON

O be not proud, though wise and fair,
Beauty's but earth, wit is but air,
As you be virtuous be not cruel,
Accept good will more than a jewel.

LADY BERKELEY

Witty, pretty, virtuous and fair,
Compounded all of fire and air,
Sweet, measure not my thought and me
By golden fruit from fruitless tree.

A PRIVATE COMMISSION

LADY STANHOPE
O Philomela fair and wise,
What means your friend to tyrannize
And make you still complain of wrong?
Henceforth his praise shall be your song,
Which none but you can sing so well,
When none his true love shall excel.

LADY COMPTON
What may be said of you and yours?
You are his joy, yours he procures:
He doth your virtue much adore,
You reverence his as much or more:
Draw where you list, for in this tree
Your fortunes cannot bettered be.

LADY FIELDING
Fie, let it never make you sad
Whether your Chance be good or bad:
If your love give but half his heart,
The devil take the other part.

MRS GRESLEY
The fruit that is so early gotten
In the eating may prove rotten,
If your love's heart do prove untrue
The fault is theirs that chose for you.

MRS PACKINGTON
In love assured, he is he
That sends this poor pale heart to thee:
As e'er you hope to be regarded,
Pray that his faith may be rewarded.

MRS K. FISCHER

Who saith thou art not fair and wise,
This paper tells him that he lies:
The worst thing that I know by thee
Is that (I fear) thou lov'st not me.

MRS SACHEVERELL

Although this heart false coloured be,
Sweet fair one, think not so of me,
For he that this your token sends
Was ever true to all his friends.

MRS M. FISCHER

Good Lord, how courteous I am grown
To give so many hearts away,
But those that I gave lost mine own:
If I had twenty none should stay.

MRS DANVERS

All evil fortune hast thou mist,
Great is the virtue of th' Amatist
If (Amatist) thou mayest say,
Then blest is such a wedding day.

MRS EGERTON

What luck had you to stay so long:
Fortune (not I) hath done you wrong,
The hearts are gone without recall,
Would I had power to please you all.

W.Sh[K]R.

The Present-givers and their Presents

THE PRESENT-GIVERS are all women or girls, and they are all neighbours or close relations of the Earl and Countess of Huntingdon of Ashby-de-la-Zouch on the border of Leicestershire and Derbyshire. This Countess was the bride's younger sister, but she had been married for six years. The ladies give their presents and recite their verses in order of precedence, Lady Derby first. The archives of the borough of Leicester record a payment for the entertainment of the Countess of Derby and Huntingdon and the Earl on 27 July 1607. The Queen's Players got 30 shillings. The hire of two horses for the Mayor and his sergeant, 'to ride on into the forest' to meet the Earl and the two Countesses hunting, was disallowed by the town council.

No members of the Brydges family, to which Lord Chandos belonged, were present, or if they were there then they were silent. There are several hints in the poems that this was a goodbye ceremony performed principally by the women of the bride's family. But Lord Chandos is a significant figure. He was born Grey Brydges in 1579 and inherited his title in 1602, aged twenty-three. His father was a close friend and supporter of the Earl of Essex, and lucky to keep his head on his shoulders after Essex's rebellion. The new Lord Chandos lived at Sudeley Castle and was called 'King of the Cotswolds'. He had a bitter family quarrel over the inheritance with his cousin Elizabeth, and it was thought he should marry her to settle it, but he refused. A few years after his marriage he was closely associated with Lord Herbert of Cherbury. He died suddenly in 1621. John Donne's friend the Countess of Bedford thought Chandos was poisoned by spa water.

Alice Derby was a daughter of Sir John Spencer of Althorpe. Her first husband, Ferdinando, Earl of Derby, died in 1594. Her second was Thomas Egerton, Lord Brackley, a Privy Councillor and Lord Chancellor (1603), whom she married in 1600. She gives a ring. The second word of her last line is hard to read, as there has been an erasure. The alternative reading would be 'share'. Whether the discomfort is loss of virginity or loss of one's old family I am not sure. It can scarcely be the loss of the ring, because that would apply to her husband's, not her mother's present, in life as in Shakespearean comedy.

The second lady is Elizabeth, Countess of Huntingdon, an Egerton by birth, younger sister of the bride. The ceremony takes place in her husband's family house at Ashby-de-la-Zouch. Her gift is perhaps a jewel in the shape of a heart.

It is curious that Spenser's *Prothalamion*, which he wrote in autumn 1596 for the double marriage of two daughters of the Earl of Worcester from Essex House, has a connection with the Huntingdon family. The fifth Earl of Worcester, formerly Lord Herbert, was married in 1571 to Elizabeth Hastings, fourth daughter of the second Earl of Huntingdon, who was therefore the mother of both brides. It is not uncommon by any means to discover that Elizabethan noble families are related by marriage, nor is it surprising that Spenser had lived at Essex House before, when it belonged to the Earl of Leicester, but the celebration of noble weddings by professional poets is not very common, and it is reasonable to suppose that a poem by Spenser published in 1597 was still remembered in 1607. The Huntingdon–Ellesmere manuscript is a text for enacting the kind of elaborate ceremony that Spenser's *Prothalamion* describes in symbolic terms. It is also fair to remark that the two bridegrooms of the *Prothalamion* were no great catch, and one of the brides was by no means young. The explanation for this may be that the Earl of Worcester was a Catholic. He was the direct ancestor of the Dukes of Beaufort, to whom he transmitted the blood of the Plantagenets and the royal arms of England, but that of course was through the male line.

The third lady is Alice's sister Elizabeth, who is married to George Carey, the second Lord Hunsdon, who after a brief interval inherited from his father the office of Lord Chamberlain to Queen Elizabeth. His father had been the Queen's first cousin. Lady Hunsdon is Lady Huntingdon's and the bride's aunt, but only Lady Huntingdon's mother takes precedence before her in her own house; Lady Hunsdon is not a Countess. Her present is a jewel but not an emblem.

The fourth lady is Lady Berkeley (Berckly). She is Lady Hunsdon's daughter, another Elizabeth, and therefore a first cousin of Lady Huntingdon and of the bride. She is married to Sir Thomas, the son of Henry, Lord Berkeley. Sir Thomas (1575–1611) did not live long enough to succeed his father, but this lady's son did so. As a boy of thirteen he was married off by his parents to a girl of nine. Elizabeth Berkeley's present is apparently a gilded or a golden apple.

The fifth present-giver is Catherine, who is married to Sir Philip Stanhope, later Lord Stanhope and finally Earl of Chesterfield. She is the Earl of Huntingdon's sister and by birth a Hastings, and therefore the bride's sister's sister-in-law. Her present seems to be a nightingale; once again I assume a piece of jewellery. The reference to tyranny is to Ovid's story about Philomela, and the complaining of wrong may mean no more than musical lamentation.

There is some uncertainty about Lady Compton, the sixth lady in the ceremony. The likeliest candidate is Elizabeth, the daughter of a Lord Mayor of London, Sir John Spencer, who came from Suffolk and was unrelated to the Spencers of

Althorpe. This lively girl had been stolen from her home in London in 1598, hidden in a baker's basket, by William, the second Lord Compton, later first Earl of Northampton. When his mean and aged father-in-law the Mayor died at last in 1610, William is said to have gone crazy for a time at the thought of all the money he had inherited. His father, Henry, the first Lord Compton, had been married to Frances, a sister of the fourth Earl of Huntingdon, which means Elizabeth Compton's mother-in-law had been the present Lady Huntingdon's great-aunt. But when Frances died, Henry Compton had married Alice Derby's sister Anne, making his son Alice's sister's stepson. William Compton and his stolen bride called their son, who grew up to be the cavalier Earl of Northampton (1601–43), Spencer Compton, but the Mayor remained obdurately furious. Queen Elizabeth is said to have calmed him down. He died leaving between half and three-quarters of a million pounds, not a penny of it to charity. Lady Compton's present is in the shape of a tree.

The seventh is Susan, Lady Fielding, married to Sir William, later Earl of Denbigh. She was a sister of the Duke of Buckingham. The Fieldings lived close to Ashby-de-la-Zouch. Her gift might be a divided heart.

Arnold Davenport connected Mrs Gresley with Susan Ferrers, who married George, son of Sir Thomas Gresley of Drakelow, just across the border in Derbyshire; Castle Gresley is even closer to Ashby-de-la-Zouch, and the eighth lady, like the seventh, is quite probably a neighbour. In 1610 the miscellany at the end of the *History and Gazetteer of Derbyshire* (Glover and Noble 1829) records a violent election quarrel and 'great affray' between Sir George Griesley and Sir Philip Stanhope. Is her present in the shape of fruit or of a heart?

Packington is even closer, just to the south of Ashby-de-la-Zouch. Davenport thought the lady may be a sister of Sir John Packington of Westwood in Worcestershire, a Privy Councillor, but the village of Packington is closer. Her present is the poor, pale heart. It seems possible that the ceremony has taken a fresh turn, and that the last seven presents, or some of them, come from the bridegroom's family. In that case, the 'early gotten' fruit of Mrs Gresley might be a strawberry, and the message might be his.

The two Mrs Fischers (Fishers) defeated Arnold Davenport. Mrs R. Fischer was born Elizabeth Tyringham and her mother was a Throckmorton. Robert Fischer lived at Packington, or Great Packington, Warwickshire; in 1607 he was twenty-eight. His father was a knight (1604) and Robert was knighted in 1609. He succeeded his father in 1619 and became a baronet in 1622. He served as Sheriff of Warwickshire. Mrs W. Fischer was probably married to Robert's younger brother, but Robert is recorded at Balliol (aged nineteen) though W. Fischer is not, so the relationship might be more remote.

The first Mrs Fischer speaks of 'this paper', and her present may be a portrait, probably a miniature, of the bride, or else it might be a mirror, in which case why the paper? Do they present their emblems and verses like the knights at the tournament in *Pericles*? The two Fischers are tenth and twelfth. The second of them seems to refer to playing cards.

The eleventh lady, Mrs Sacheverell, is Elizabeth, married to Jacinth Sacheverell of Morley in Derbyshire, not far away. Her father was Sir Richard Harpur and her uncle Sir John of Swerkston in Derbyshire (north of Ashby), to whom Marston refers in a letter about his masque. He is writing to Sir George Clifton, apologizing for not having sent a copy:

> First with my own hand I wrote one copy; for all the rest which I had caused to be transcribed were given and stolen from me at my Lord Spencer's. Then with all sudden care I gave my copy unto a scrivener to write out, who is now upon it and will instantly have ended it.

Lord Spencer is Alice Derby's brother Robert, the first Lord Spencer of Althorpe. Sir Gervase was probably one of the knights in the masque. I have considered and rejected the idea that the masque itself was at Ashby House, as its manuscript says it was, but the ceremony of presents was at Althorpe, Lord Spencer's house in Northamptonshire, because that is too far south to favour the Gresley, Packington, Drakelow and Swerkston neighbours so well, or the recorded visit of Alice Derby to the Huntingdons. Marston must have gone south with her to her family house at Althorpe, where naturally the Spencer family will have wanted copies of the masque done at Ashby. The present-givers, like the masquers, were at Ashby: Alice Derby's visit to her daughter's house was combined with a family ceremony for her other daughter's engagement, which was performed chiefly by those women of her family who could be mustered there. Mrs Sacheverell gives an enamelled heart. Once again it is sent by Chandos.

The thirteenth lady is perhaps one of the Danvers family of Dauntsey in Wiltshire, one of whom became the Earl of Danby. Davenport prefers the wife of a Middle Temple man from Culworth in Leicestershire. George Herbert's mother, Magdalen, who died in 1627, married Sir John Danvers, and George Herbert himself met and married Jane Danvers at Dauntsey in 1629. She was one of the daughters of Charles Danvers of Brynton. They seem a likelier family than the Leicestershire lawyer's, but this is quite a humble lady, far down the list. She brings or gives an amethyst. The spelling 'amatist' may imply a Latin pun about love based on a similar pun in Virgil.

The last lady is an Egerton, and Davenport's clever idea that she is a small girl is surely right. The first and last poems are particularly outspoken. She would be a tiny granddaughter of Alice Derby. Alice's second daughter Frances married her half-brother Sir John Egerton early in 1602, so this would be a little Egerton girl aged four or five. Double marriages of that kind were intended to secure succession to property. If Mrs Egerton is a child, perhaps she gives nothing, or the empty basket. The point about 'stay so long' is that Anne Chandos was at least twenty-six. She was a Stanley, not an Egerton, eldest daughter of the Earl of Derby. The marriage, arranged no doubt with some difficulty due to her father's death, finally took place early in 1608.